JOHNSON/BURGEE:ARCHITECTURE

JOHNSON

THE BUILDINGS AND PROJECTS OF
PHILIP JOHNSON AND JOHN BURGEE

BURGEE:ARCHITECTURE

TEXT BY NORY MILLER
PHOTOGRAPHS BY RICHARD PAYNE

THE ARCHITECTURAL PRESS: LONDON

ALL PHOTOGRAPHS ARE BY RICHARD PAYNE EXCEPT
THE COLOR PHOTOGRAPHS ON PAGES 40 AND 41 BY DAVID FRANZEN,
THE PHOTOGRAPHS ON PAGES 110 AND 111 BY HARR-HEDRICH BLESSING, AND
THE PHOTOGRAPHS ON PAGES 114 AND 115 BY LOUIS CHECKMAN

FIRST PUBLISHED IN GREAT BRITAIN IN 1980 BY THE ARCHITECTURAL PRESS LTD.,
9 QUEEN ANNE'S GATE, LONDON SW1H 9BY.
ISBN 085139 544 9

MANUFACTURED BY AMILCARE PIZZI, S.P.A., MILAN, ITALY
98765432
FIRST EDITION

CONTENTS

INTRODUCTION

Johnson and Burgee met fifteen years ago during an interview for a commission they didn't get. Philip Johnson was already a well-known architect as well as a highly regarded architectural historian and curator. John Burgee was a partner with the large Chicago firm of C. F. Murphy Associates. What they formed was an unusual partnership, one in which both members not only design, but design together. The result has been the best work in either of their careers, the receipt of every award that is given to architects and some that aren't, and international attention for more than a decade.

They have been standard-bearers without an army. There is no school of Johnson/Burgee, nor followers in any direct sense of the word. But few of their buildings have not been the fulcrum of debate within the profession, the schools and even the general public. They have challenged a number of prevailing notions about architecture and shown up others as contradictory. In doing so, they have questioned the core of modernist thought. They have abandoned not simply the particular stylistic aspects of modernist architecture, such as buildings with flat tops, but the inherent if unspoken presumption that the forms of modernist architecture are to be architecture's final solution. Their dismissal of the necessity of the forms is a dismissal of the foundation upon which the theory is based: that human nature and social organization can be perfected through these forms.

If Johnson and Burgee have sometimes been called the most sincerely hated architects in the world, it is because they scoff at what many of their fellows still regard as a higher moral purpose. "The day of ideology is thankfully over; let us celebrate the death of the <u>idée fixe</u>," says Johnson. That their buildings are quite functional, hold up well over time, show a predilection for material honesty—all tenets of modernism—is overshadowed. It is their iconoclasm that has been influential.

What Johnson/Burgee substitutes for the belief that architecture is reformatory is the sure knowledge that it is a perceptual experience. This is the architects' standard, one which Johnson has carried for decades but one which has had its greatest impact from the work of the partnership.

The buildings have been investigations of those sensate elements that transform shelter into occasion. It is an investigation informed by a thorough knowledge of architecture of past ages and sculpture of this age. And it is an investigation so far-ranging that continuity is much more easily recognized in detail than at first impression.

Formally the architects have been working their way out of the abstraction that was called for by modernism's "<u>Sachlichkeit</u>" (objectivity), with a deliberateness that was sometimes missing from Johnson's earlier but equally rebellious work. Although the forms and sources change, the direction has been consistently toward articulation and vividness. Modernism's neutral exterior skin becomes wall; doorway becomes entry; flat tops become carved finials; right-angled containers become shapes; empty slab plazas become lively galleries.

Johnson and Burgee are hardly alone in this quest, and they have learned as much from their contemporaries as they have taught them. What makes the firm unique is that its efforts have taken place in large-scale, highly visible work. If the debate about modernism has moved out of the tight academic circles, where such debates invariably begin, into a matter of public concern, it is, to a large extent, Johnson/Burgee that put it there.   N. M.

JOHNSON/BURGEE:ARCHITECTURE

ART MUSEUM OF SOUTH TEXAS

CORPUS CHRISTI, TEXAS

Corpus Christi is a city of about a quarter million people living almost exclusively off oil wells and refineries on the Gulf of Mexico near the Mexican border. The cultural institutions in town—the only ones for more than a hundred miles—sit together, a short walk from downtown, on the edge of Corpus Christi Bay. Johnson/Burgee designed the art museum, a small low-budget building that makes very much out of very little.

The tools are elementary: thick walls of white concrete so carefully crafted that it rivals marble; rich bronze trimming; primary forms; and familar images like colonial houses, village squares, pueblos, bridges, Spanish missions, courtyards. They are employed with sophistication: overlap, reversal, framing, scale shifts, disjuncture, crystallized polarities played out against one another.

The moment of entry is caught between easy approachability and passage into a different world. The façade both assembles into a recognizable house, with pitched roof, recessed attic and massive chimney (actually the staircase), and dissolves into stark-white hard-edged shapes set slightly ajar from one another. Formality of occasion is indicated by the immense unrolled concrete carpet which in its exaggerated scale shrinks the museum back into a little building. The doorway is a gaping black hole leading directly into a double-height great hall, around which the rooms are disposed eccentrically. A forerunner of the firm's village-square plans, the hall is both gallery and lobby, and doubles for receptions and formal dinners, since the building is as much community center as museum. "We had to make the building look like something, even though it was small," says Johnson, "so all the elements got broken apart."

The portals to rooms and out-of-doors are exaggerated, and unique spaces like the auditorium are distinctively shaped. Each gallery is approached by an elaborate and protracted pathway that heightens the sense of anticipation, going under trestles, across bridges and up a hidden sunlit cylindrical staircase. Unity is provided through material, a white aggregate in white cement. "Part of my philosophy," says Burgee, "is that if you can't afford the best wood, use the best plastic. But never use the scrap of any material. We couldn't afford the best marble, so we used the best concrete."

The magic of the museum lies in the inventive fashioning of light and view. The climate of Corpus Christi suggested to the architects the Mediterranean as well as the American Southwest. They drew on both traditions—the reflective white stucco walls and courtyards of Mikonos and the heavy adobe with punched windows of the Navajo. The museum is an escape from the climate; quiet, shaded and cool. Where the architects introduce openings, they do so with visual ingenuity. Opposite the front door there is a huge painting of a ship on the ocean. Except that the ship is moving, and it's not a painting, it's a view outdoors through a man-size window. It is stagecraft in the best sense of the baroque, and to the right it is augmented by a second window recessed in its own small alcove like a private screening. Above each window and door is an enchanted garden. Suspended weightlessly over fragile glass, brilliant with sunshine, these shallow balconies provide most of the color and all of the softness in the building.

Part of the magic is to reverse conventional understandings of inside and outside. Although the openings to the street, courtyards and seashore are the accepted links to outdoors, their gray tint inserts a filmy barrier, while clearly interior spaces, lit by skylights, are brighter.

It is a building that derives its presence not from size or ornateness, but from the vividness of the artistic experience, from the immediacy of things like the relation of parts to whole, solid to void, interior to exterior, image to object. At the same time, it remains an effective, neutral background for the display of art.

Inside, the Corpus Christi museum is a retreat from the Southwestern sun. Windows and doors are glazed in gray tinted glass. Sunlight from skylights is reflected brightly back and forth off the white concrete walls.

Outside, the forms are fragmented to give the small museum an unexpected impact. The forms evoke a number of associations — Spanish missions, Colonial chimneys, cave entrances, grand stairways — none of which is so specific as to deny the others.

BURDEN HALL

HARVARD UNIVERSITY
BOSTON, MASSACHUSETTS

Johnson/Burgee has done a number of auditoriums, sometimes within other designers' buildings, sometimes within its own. Burden Hall is the only one which is simply auditorium, plus a few seminar rooms, and nothing else. It is also that elusive and difficult building type, the flexible space.

Harvard University's School of Business Administration wanted an auditorium large enough to seat the entire student body, then estimated at 1,000, but since that was needed only once each term, also suitable for subdivision into smaller spaces for class and lecture. The architects had seen this type of structure before, generally a slice-of-pie shape with much of the audience back against the crust. They flattened the typical plan into a squat fan—a theater in the half-round—with never more than fifteen rows of seating and, on one side, as few as nine. The hall, which remains the largest on the Harvard campus, can be left whole or divided in thirds with movable soundproof partitions.

Thus some measure of intimacy was gained on the inside. However, there still remained the problem of reducing, or at least taming, this enormous bulk on the outside. As windows were not welcome, the architects drove the greater part of the building underground and rendered what remained above in Harvard brick. The walls are, then, casually bent in and out around the various interior functions, forming twenty-two sides in all.

In 1972, inflected volumes (what Johnson self-deprecatingly calls "the zogs") were the most anyone could think of to relieve mass if there was no window pattern or structural grid to play with. It is tempting to consider how Burden Hall would look if it had been designed with all the textural and organizational possibilities of ornament to which Johnson/Burgee turned in later work.

NEUBERGER MUSEUM

STATE UNIVERSITY OF NEW YORK
PURCHASE, NEW YORK

The State University of New York at Purchase, a cherished project of the late Governor Nelson Rockefeller, was to be a standard of college planning and design. It was an attempt to integrate modern buildings into a unified campus plan similar to the traditional buildings of Oxford or Harvard. Special design rules were laid down by master planner Edward Larrabee Barnes. Some of the leading architects, among them Venturi and Rauch, Paul Rudolph, Gunner Birkerts and Gwathmey and Siegel were involved. Johnson/Burgee was hired to do the art museum.

The requirements of the campus plan meant a museum unlike any of the eight museums (ten counting private galleries) that Johnson had done before. It had to be long and thin, flanked by pedestrian promenades separating one fingerlike building from another. It had to be sheathed in brown brick and gray glass. And it had to face onto a central paved mall lined with an "organizing" covered arcade that screened any façade the building might have. It was neither possible nor desirable to produce a community landmark, as the firm had at Corpus Christi. Here the task was to provide as pleasant, as flexible and as much space as could be achieved.

The architects describe the building as a crankshaft. There are five 60-foot-wide sections that slide back and forth like building blocks. Their overlap forms an interior street down the entire 300-foot length. The heights and numbers of stories of each block vary to provide a range of gallery spaces and to accommodate other functions in upper floors. It is all very clean, very clear, very matter-of-fact. Altogether the galleries, each one different, contain as much hanging space as the Whitney Museum. The fourth block is one of the largest individual gallery spaces in the country—90 feet by 60 feet with a 22-foot ceiling—for which several artists have been commissioned to create special works.

The crankshaft leaves courtyards along both sides, which are planted, displayed with sculpture and enclosed, each in its own way. From the inside these courtyards provide natural light, a splash of greenery, a change of pace. From the outdoor promenades they are sheltered, intimate resting places with views of the exhibits inside.

But for all the workaday quality of this building, there exist unmistakable imprints of the architects. Not only is the circulation path clear, it is marked. The front door is recessed behind the pervading brick façade of the campus, and the recess is wrapped in metal. Hung from its soffit is a wooden baffle. This deep eggcrate of stained-oak boards continues above the foyer and reappears each time an "entrance" occurs: over the stairs to the permanent collection with sunlight pouring through, on the ceiling of each elevator lobby, and just inside the back doors. The metal band becomes the repeating motif of transition between one building block and the next.

The galleries themselves bear the mark of Johnson/Burgee's long impatience with modern blank wall museums. The partners' taste leans toward the definition that traditional wainscoting and moldings give to a wall, and Purchase is a compromise between that and contemporary taste for neutrality. The walls of the galleries, like the floors, are finished in brick, rugged and of a piece with the exterior. But on each wall, held just within its dimensions, are large planes of white wallboard to set off and, the architects feel, to display properly the works of art.

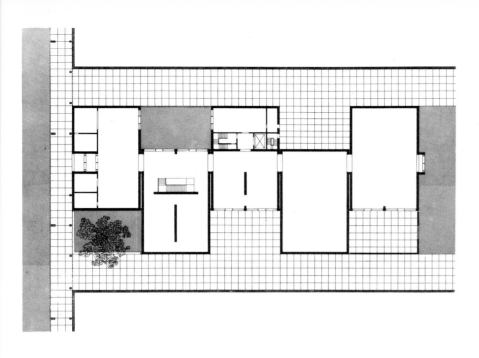

A working museum for an arts campus, the Neuberger Museum is organized for maximum flexibility. Each of its five different areas lends itself to different types of exhibits. The rear area (below) has a large proportion of floor space, suited best for sculpture or performance, and a view through the back doors onto a Revolutionary-period cemetery. Another (right) contains two smaller spaces, without natural light, and, upstairs, the Roy P. Neuberger permanent collection. An extremely large gallery space (overleaf) has motivated several artists to design work specifically for it.

I.D.S. CENTER

MINNEAPOLIS, MINNESOTA

Some buildings, significant at the time they are built, remain significant years later. Occasionally that significance has to do not only with such a building and the town in which it stands but with the way a whole country suddenly visualizes possibilities. Investors Diversified Services (I.D.S.) does this. As American architects wrestled with the progressive impoverishment of their center cities for a decade or more, broad plazas, monumental sculptures and not-very-Trevi-like fountains became a concomitant of commercial towers. In the translation from the Italian, however, much was lost to climate and lifestyle. I.D.S., even from its announcement, became the symbol of an alternative (this time owing more to northern Italy): a bustling galleria, buttressed in this American version not by cafés but by large-scale development.

For Johnson/Burgee it was an introduction to big-time commercial work. Philip Johnson had done large-scale designs before, but they had been for cultural and educational institutions. His one office-block commission had been his association with Ludwig Mies van der Rohe on the Seagram Building in New York in the fifties. With John Burgee's extensive commercial background, the new direction became feasible. The architects had, in fact, been involved in a number of planned but never built large-scale revitalization projects for other cities when I.D.S. came to them. This project was to be followed by a series of some of the most highly acclaimed commercial buildings of the decade.

As has long been typical for Johnson and remains typical of Johnson/Burgee, a new building type became an opportunity to consider what they found insufficient in stock architectural responses and to experiment with modifications. Thus the famous Crystal Court evolved. When I.D.S. approached the firm to do a downtown office tower in Minneapolis, Burgee talked them into a more complicated mixed-use project encompassing a full block. The block was favorably located on semipedestrian Nicollet Mall, surrounded by department stores and other magnets and easily interlocked into Minneapolis' skyways, a system of second-level bridges between buildings. What Johnson/Burgee did was scatter the various buildings to the corners, leave a good-sized pocket in the middle (20,000 square feet of Crystal Court), surround that court with activity and connect it to street and skyway. "The plaza is dead," declared Johnson; "long live the climate-controlled court." Especially, they thought, in a city whose climate they compared, not too unfairly, to Siberia's.

The architects then made every effort to make the court an attraction. Funnel entrances lead in from each street, and above them are the glass-enclosed bridges from neighboring buildings. Shops line the interior of both levels, and the levels are connected by a very visible escalator. Restaurants jut into the court from hotel balconies, and flowers, trees and benches brighten the ground level. Most of all, there is a sense of activity in the architecture itself. None of the entrances line up opposite one another. The court is an irregular polygon, and the walls glitter with mirrored saw-toothed zigs and zags reflecting one another at a furious pace. Piling up overhead in a jumbled pyramid are clusters of giant ice cubes of glass and plastic that give this space its name, a canopy that rises at its highest point to 121 feet and through which can be seen the soaring inclines of the towers. Surrounding the court are the fifty-one-story I.D.S. headquarters, an eight-story annex, a two-story Woolworth's and a hotel rising sixteen stories over a three-story bank. Parking is underground.

If the court is Johnson/Burgee's break with the Lever House tower-and-plaza tradition, the buildings are the first of a series which were to challenge the formula of the glass office tower. To visually reduce the bulk of what was to be the tallest building in town, they made the shape not rectangular, but octagonal. The diagonal sides are splintered into eight setbacks that fracture the reflections of clouds, city skyline and one another. True to Mies's glass boxes, but by no means

typical of the genre, the architects organized the tower classically into base, shaft and capital. Mechanical floors, as at the Seagram Building, function as the capital but also serve to mark a distinction between the tower adjacent to the court and the tower as it rises alone. Nor does the exterior wall conform to the formula. As it was to be sheathed in chrome-coated reflective glass, the architects felt that efforts must be made to keep it from becoming utterly scaleless. They chose as transparent a material as they could afford. Mullions were set twice as close to one another as normal. "I'm sick of the five-foot module," Johnson explained, and described the result of this 2-foot, 6-inch module as a birdcage.

Like the breaking of the box at I.D.S., the manipulation of the curtain wall was the first of what became, and continues to be, a major preoccupation of the firm. The organization of the complex itself, however, is a concept that the firm has applied before in a wide variety of building types: that is, the organization of a building as if it were the center of a city. This time it is as much reality as metaphor. Nicollet Mall is the center of Minneapolis, and I.D.S. is the center of Nicollet Mall. For this center Johnson/Burgee sifted through the qualities of medieval town planning, suburban shopping malls, bazaars, New England villages, Roman houses, contemporary hotels and many more. The crystal court is part city square, part shopping center, part atrium, part lobby, part old-fashioned market. It is a place for contemporary urban Americans to gather.

The architects referred to the Crystal Court as the town square, but its crystalline roof gave it the name it is known by. The idea of a covered galleria surrounded by buildings grew out of Minneapolis' harsh climate. The court became a seminal building in the popular imagination for this alternative to open plazas.

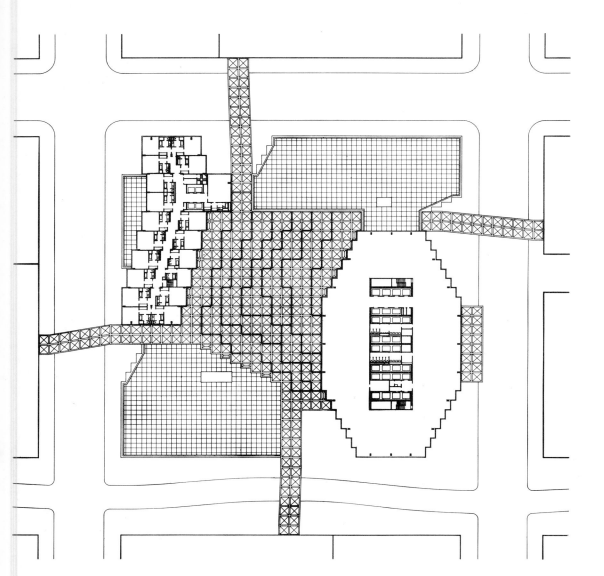

The variety of building types and scales of I.D.S. Center share a common geometric motif: the faceted plane. It is used to fracture the mass of the tall headquarters, to stagger the rooms of the hotel, and to give separate identity to the row of shops. It is the faceting of the ceiling and mirrored walls of the Crystal Court that makes it seem bustling whether it is crowded or relatively empty.

I.D.S. was Johnson/Burgee's first experiment in how to inflect a mirrored glass building to avoid scalelessness. The strategy was twofold: exaggerate the frame in which the mirrored panels are set, and break down the overall mass. The stepped-back edges had the added advantage of providing thirty-two corner offices per floor.

BOSTON PUBLIC LIBRARY ADDITION

BOSTON, MASSACHUSETTS

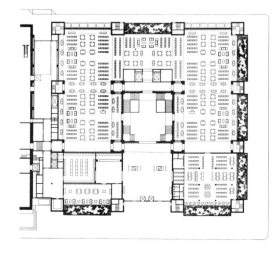

By the late 1950s, Philip Johnson was discouraged by how badly modern architecture fit into older-style university campuses and downtowns. He had begun to suggest in speeches which were considered highly inflammatory that architects might consider copying the earlier styles for such commissions rather than follow the modernist dictum to strike anew. The addition to the Boston Public Library gave him the opportunity to test his words.

The original library, in Boston's Back Bay, is one of McKim, Mead & White's best pieces, built in 1888–1895 in Renaissance revival style with a sumptuous marble staircase and finely scaled courtyard. As a nineteenth-century library, however, it was burdened by closed bookstacks and geared to a nineteenth-century population. The city came to Philip Johnson in 1964 for an addition. The project changed several times and ultimately took nine years to finish (during which time Burgee became Johnson's partner). By completion it was larger than the original building, with eight floors aboveground and two below, next-door to the old library and connected inside by an umbilical corridor.

The exterior shocked critics and fellow architects alike. The roof is a direct copy of McKim's, so that from afar the addition seems a contemporary continuation. Said Johnson at the time: "The pitched roof is a feature that normally I would never use; compromise is necessary when building a wing onto an older building." The architects faced the addition in the same granite as the original, having reopened the quarry to do so. They modeled the façade to hold the cornice line of McKim's library as well as continue its strong horizontal string courses, albeit translated in form.

Where the addition differs from the 1895 building is in the grain of its detail. The architects felt that such a delicately ornamented façade was no longer affordable and no longer appropriate to the long-span structural systems of modern construction. Instead of the narrow-spaced arches of the revival building, Johnson/Burgee divided the new façade vertically into three enormous bays (corresponding to the divisions of structure and interior space).

The architects set the addition slightly off from the old library in a deliberate gesture of deference, but the bold scale of the new structure has an assertiveness of its own. The irony is that a building thought outrageously revivalist when it was built should only a few years later be criticized, as it has been, for being not revivalist enough. It is a solid measure of the impact both the design and its architects have had.

The huge interior space (230 feet by 252 feet) is divided into more manageable areas by its nine-square plan, a regulating device Johnson explains that he "got" from J.-N.-L. Durand's <u>Précis des Leçons</u>, a volume that had served virtually as a textbook of romantic classicism in the nineteenth century.

The nine-square plan results in three bays on each façade and one square locked in the middle. This central square has become the reference point for the whole building. Left open for all eight levels, it is fully 60 feet high and lit from above through glass skylights, which repeat the nine-square theme. Johnson said: "In my design approach, second only to the clarity of circulation is the monumentality of a central space. This monumental space should be symbolic of the devotion to the Muses, inherent in a public library." The word "monumentality" was a red flag to many of his colleagues, as was the "anti-functionalism" of a whole bay on each floor that stored neither people nor books. It was a red flag Johnson had waved many times before, at Lincoln Center and his early museums, though the Boston library addition was the last time he was to wave it with such solemnity.

Johnson/Burgee's addition employs a different vocabulary than does the original Boston Public Library, but major façade divisions and the roof shape match. For the new library, the most striking features are the huge lunette windows of the reading rooms. Inside, the plan revolves around a central court open to the top floor and roofed in glass.

NIAGARA FALLS CONVENTION CENTER

NIAGARA FALLS, NEW YORK

The Niagara Falls Convention Center involved the firm in a major urban renewal venture, as had I.D.S. The American half of the twin honeymoon cities had been losing tourists and citizens for a decade or so and had watched its once elegant downtown grow irreparably seedy. In 1969 the city interested the state Urban Development Corporation, and began an 82-acre urban renewal project that is still under way. The plan includes office buildings, a hotel, shopping center, winter garden, parking garages and museum. It was the role of the convention center not only to attract business to Niagara Falls but to play a crucial part in the creation of a strong visual impact to downtown.

The axis of the renewal area is a 1,500-foot-long tree-lined pedestrian mall, bordered on part of one side by a two-level arcade with shops behind. It is off this axis that the various new buildings are arranged. At the Niagara River end, the mall runs into a riverside park and the most dramatic view of the waterfall. The convention center was to anchor the other end of the mall. It does so in the tradition of a triumphal arch, or perhaps the domed pantheon. A huge building, it is all sweeping curve that stretches from beyond one side of the mall to beyond the other. The view down the mall is of a vast glass quarter moon on a plinth of stone, the centralized form not only finishing the view but providing a focus for the perspective. Part of the building extends on to the mall itself, forming a canopy over the street—a street which cars use not only to drop off passengers but also as an avenue through town. "Too many convention centers are places where only out-of-towners come and enjoy themselves," says Burgee. "This is a part of the life of the natives, a symbol of their city pulling itself up by its bootstraps."

Within, the building is divided into a huge glassy arched space above the first story in the center, and limestone-clad feet at the edges. The central hall, an attempt to recapture something of the grandeur of old railroad stations with the technology of the airplane hangar, is classic universal space. Left alone, it is a 100,000-square-foot exhibition hall. Up to 6,000 tiered seats can be inserted, making it a temporary arena used for a variety of other events. Between the canted walls of the main hall and the points at which the tips of the arc touch the ground are a series of ancillary spaces: a 2,000-person ballroom, a 400-seat thrust stage theater, large and small meeting rooms, kitchens and storage among them.

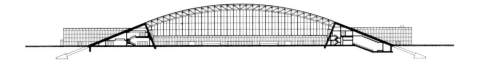

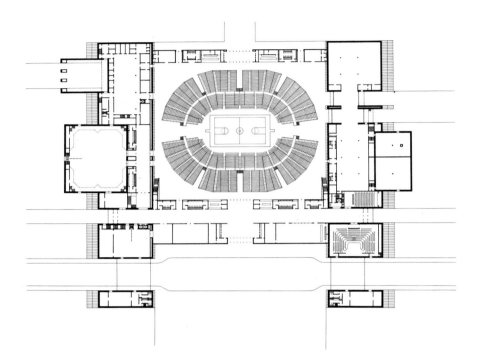

Johnson/Burgee found the typical solution to a convention center — "a barn in back of an arena," as Burgee puts it — untenable in terms of circulation. Their Niagara Convention Center combines both exhibition and coliseum function in one space with demountable seats. A variety of other uses, such as a small theater (below left) as well as ballrooms and meeting rooms, are accommodated at the edges.

FORT WORTH WATER GARDEN

FORT WORTH, TEXAS

One of Johnson/Burgee's major encounters with designing landscape, the water garden, was an extraordinary commission. The local Amon Carter Foundation bought a four-and-one-half-block site in a deteriorating edge of Fort Worth's downtown, hired the architects, gave them few restrictions, and then donated the park to its city. In an era of vest-pocket parks and plazas, this was a respite from the city big enough to wander in. And the architects programed that wandering with pathways, wayside stops, events and hideaways to draw out the experience, to convey more of the sense of a Central Park or Villa d'Este than its limited acreage would have suggested possible.

What they created was a miniature landscape of mountains, forests and lakes in the image of an architect's contour map. They maintained an extreme economy of means—tan-colored concrete, greenery and water—and manipulated these few elements within a restrictive geometric order. Within those limits, however, the architects set about introducing every type and shade of variety that could be squeezed in. Layers of concrete edges and soft plantings pile up quickly for mountains or more gradually as cultivated hillsides. Sometimes stone ridges step up like an Aztec pyramid or erupt in groves of oak, ginkgo and gum. Everywhere there are widened spaces tucked inside the mountains in which to sit and to read or to think. There is constant variation of lushness and hardness, simpler and more frenetic configurations, height and depth. There are so many vectors of movement that it is intriguing and animated and vivid, but the palette is so restricted that it never loses continuity.

The mountains form the edge and the webbing of the water garden. Paths lead from the sidewalks down to the central plaza. The underlying geometric framework involves the same grid shift as at I.D.S., but instead of buildings distributed around a pentagonal plaza, there are natural settings. Some are quite public, some are hidden. The most dramatic is the grand waterfall, a public event just off the plaza and visible from the street. Cliffs of water cascade from all sides, at all different speeds, with all different sounds, over narrower and wider steps into the center pit. Here a pentagonal dam threads the water through more than twenty narrow channels, churning into a froth at the very bottom. It is a kaleidoscope of sound and light and total motion, all of which changes as one moves around it. One wildly unruly spill suddenly seems to have stopped altogether, while the sudsing rapids next to it (similarly quiet a few footsteps ago) are as agitated as they were previously still. Down the middle of this white-water gorge is a series of benchlike steps that the brave and foolhardy are invited to take.

Close to the plaza, but a complete surprise to the wanderer who has turned and turned again along a narrow woodsy trail, is a "dancing pool." Almost forty jets spurt straight up, the water collecting in a hovering feathery mist and falling back in little droplets, lending a continuous sparkle to the surface. The sunken lake, visible from above over low balconies, is an irregular seven-sided basin next to a raised platform and lined with trees inside high angled walls. One balcony's banister is water, which washes down the polygonal interior of this sacred precinct. While open to view, it is not so open to access. There are only two stairways, concealed from many viewpoints, and to descend is to enter narrow slits between high walls. Only at the bottom, when the stairs end and one has been turned almost halfway around, is the pool visible again. In the process it has been transformed, from a dramatic cavity to a cool and protected place of contemplation.

Around the top of the sunken pool are small plateaus, an amphitheater in an outside corner, and a winding little path to the street that leads to a completely unexpected flower garden instead. Banked flower beds, grassy mounds and a solid line of trees hold out against the adjacent highway as best they can for the softest part of the park.

From the outside, the low mountains and an occasional glimpse of the grand waterfall are the clues that in the midst of the traffic lights and decaying buildings and some of the least convincing modern architecture imaginable, there is an urban park the scope of which hadn't been seen in decades.

One of the largest downtown parks of its decade, Fort Worth largely eschews the usual meadows and forests for a series of water events. The grand waterfall (right) is the most elaborate. Distributed around the park are an amphitheater overlooking a flower garden, a sunken lake (above) and a mist pool (overleaf).

MORNINGSIDE HOUSE

NEW YORK, NEW YORK

Morningside House is a rare moment for Johnson/Burgee: the one time the firm has taken on the little understood and always underfinanced task of either public housing or health care. The firm's response is straightforward, practical and urban. The project is a church-sponsored, partially state-financed nursing home for the elderly on two odd-shaped sites across the street from each other. The architects treated the sites separately and built two buildings. Each is a double-loaded corridor that curls around like a worm, arching up to its street corner on one side and embracing a protected pocket on the other. Shielded from traffic and strangers, these inner courts become places to plant gardens, play shuffle-board and socialize outdoors.

Concrete alternates with ribbon windows on the exterior. The windows are tinted gray and set deep, partly to inject some play of light and shadow into this recalcitrant bulk, partly to conserve energy and partly to conceal their unavoidably inexpensive detailing. Various adjustments are then made in this basic pattern. The concrete bends stiffly around corners, the windows glide on by, leaving triangular gaps at each of a handful of corners. These become delicately railed balconies onto the street. Where elevators and stairs occur, the concrete simply fills in, giving some vertical thrust to the long, low buildings. For the first story, the concrete skirt is raised higher for privacy with only a thin clerestory line of light.

There is little of procession here except for the two entrances. These are inserted into the wall as foreign objects—glass doors surrounded by glass panes—and then covered with thin concrete canopies, which the architects have deftly slipped out of the clerestory ribbon above. The entrances are not directly across from each other—an attempt, along with the nonrectilinear geometry of the plan, to enliven the composition.

PENNZOIL PLACE

HOUSTON, TEXAS

Pennzoil Place takes the ideas and forms of I.D.S. and simplifies, condenses and extends them. Economy of means, dictated by the material situation, emerged as the point of the aesthetic. Johnson and Burgee, admirers of minimalist sculpture as they had become critics of overly minimal office buildings, found in Pennzoil the opportunity to transfer the lessons of the one into the terms of the other. Johnson's own satisfaction with the result is unmistakable. He calls it "the most successful sculpture that John Burgee and I have built."

Pennzoil Company board chairman J. Hugh Liedtke initiated the project but went to Texas developer Gerald D. Hines to put it together. It began as something between a corporate headquarters and speculative real estate, but when a second major tenant was found, the Zapata Corporation, the project became a hybrid that needed a double identity. Liedtke further emphasized, to the architects' obvious relief, that he didn't "want just another building," particularly not an "upended cigar box." And when an early model was brought to him, he objected to the typically International Style flat roof, declaring that he wanted the building "to soar, to reach, and a flat top doesn't reach."

Pennzoil is as distinctive on Houston's skyline as I.D.S. is on Minneapolis', despite its being shorter than several of its neighbors. It is distinctive because it is slanted on top, sides and bottom; because the closeness of color between its bronze-tinted glass and bronze-anodized aluminum as well as the severity of its geometry gives it a starkness unmatched by anything around; and because void as well as solid is tightened so resolutely in place as to exact the one quality that distinguishes fine art from attractiveness—tension.

The site is a full block with a circulation path slicing through it diagonally and two thirty-six-story towers rising opposite each other, one named for Pennzoil, the other for the Zapata Corporation. The point of intersection between them, their 135-degree corners, are held just 10 feet apart, an architectural high-wire act that is as exciting to view from surrounding highways (the buildings slip together and apart in an imaginary square dance) as it is from directly underneath. The tops of the towers are simply sliced right off at a 45-degree angle, which Burgee describes as a "traditional gable roof, half on each building." In one stroke Liedtke got his soaring top, distinctive image and extraordinary executive offices, with all of the light and some of the nostalgia of an artist's garret.

From the pitched roofs, the towers descend uniformly to the ground, embellished only slightly by the subtle bands of windows and spandrels and the opposing spines of the projecting and continuous vertical mullions, set close together. Except, that is, at their bases. The materials, color and thickness of the curtain walls remain the same for these bases, but the rhythm changes from its narrow module to a jazzlike improvisation of single, double and triple widths. As bottom, middle and top are not blurred together in a modernist enthusiasm for inarticulate skin, neither is the venerable corner allowed merely to occur. Johnson once said about the corner: "It is, next to the cornice or top, the most sensitive part of a design. Schinkel and Mies share the same approach; slow down your fenestration rhythm, introduce an element, a column, a pilaster, that will tie your building to the ground and at the same time cut off your horizontal elements."

Only three quarters of the site is used for office towers. The rest is a circulation path in the shape of two triangles, roofed over and set tip-to-tip between the buildings as a high-tech galleria. "In a city," Johnson reiterates, "what's left over in front outside has no meaning." There are commercial banks inside and a shopping and restaurant concourse below, connected to Houston's extensive tunnel system. Its roof is a pyramid of white truss work and glass that looks like mesh pulled tight between the towers from outside and an erector-set pit against the elements from within.

Pennzoil's galleria is a shortcut through the site as well as a covered plaza. Trees, flowers and sunlight give it the feel of outdoors. Along the sides are commercial banks and the entries to the elevator lobbies of the towers.

The two spaces—galleria and tower lobbies—are kept quite distinct. One is pulled into the galleria by the enormous converging lines of its disappearing greenhouse roof, by the rude gash in its perfect form, by the fattest, most self-conscious rain trough ever affixed and, on one side, by two columnar pylons.

The tower entrances are marked far less dramatically by canopies and layered rows of lights. The interiors of the tower lobbies have a shadowy light thrown from hidden coves, making the granite walls seem as soft as carpet. The galleria, in contrast, bursts with sunlight. Covered in glass, flanked by mirrored reflections and lushly planted at its edges, it is less a room than a park. A few large-scale versions of I.D.S.'s jagged edges are tried here for liveliness. Such architectural necessities as elevators and escalators to the concourse level are treated as big pieces of street furniture, in polished granite.

Pennzoil Place makes many of the same departures from the conventional glass box as did I.D.S., but in one respect, the top, it goes further; and in another, its silhouette, it is better. It is another variation on overall form and curtain-wall patterning. Its climate-controlled court off the sidewalk, if less of a busy town square than that at I.D.S., does offer the kind of public/private lingering once available along the shop-lined lobbies of great urban hotels. And Pennzoil does all this for a construction price that was just slightly above the mean at the time— more to the point, a number that still allowed the building to be 97 percent pre-leased at completion, with two extra floors added in the middle to keep up with demand.

When it was finished, the building was hailed by a number of critics as the building of the year because it proved all the things that the critics wanted proved. It showed that office buildings don't have to look as if they have all been stamped from the same mold; that skyscrapers could offer more at street level than elevators; and most of all, that this could be accomplished at a cost even speculative developers would be willing to pay.

Minimalist sculpture was the source for Pennzoil's break with the classic glass box. The building's powerful shape is recognizable from great distances despite its moderate height.

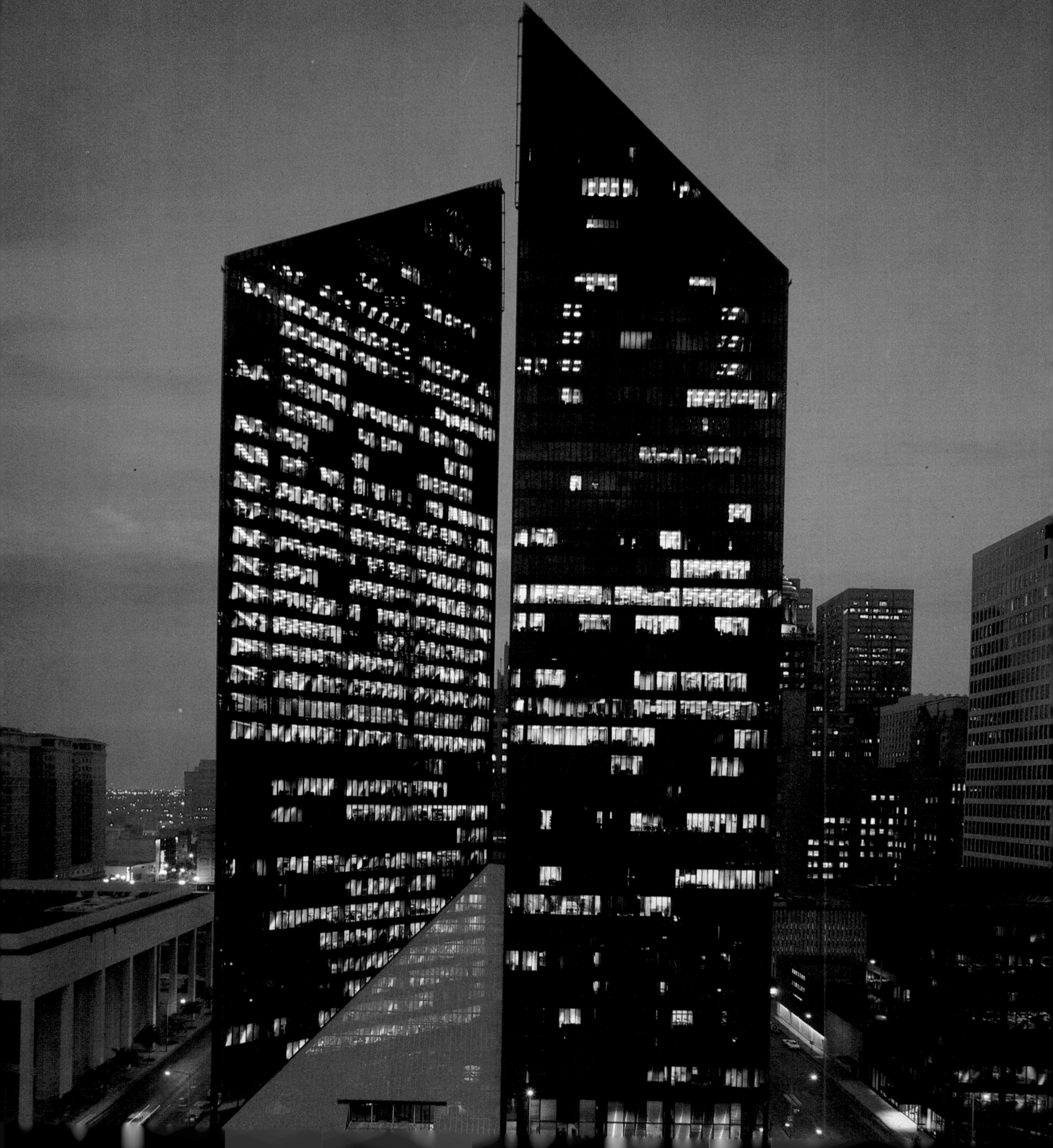

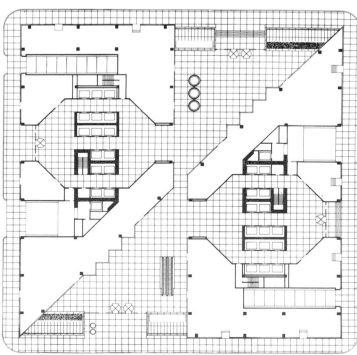

As the faceted wall was to I.D.S., so is the slanted wall to Pennzoil. The gallerias have a slanted edge (above), and the two towers each have a slanted side and top.

POST OAK CENTRAL I & II

HOUSTON, TEXAS

Johnson's "one cannot not know history" is taken more or less literally in all of the firm's work, but rarely as literally as at Post Oak Central. At the doorway to these suave moderne towers with their slippery curves and shimmering surfaces, Myrna Loy could be waiting for William Powell to pick her up in a Cord. In the actual 1930s, art deco and art moderne were more threatening golden calves to Johnson's hopes of legitimizing the International Style in the United States than even the Beaux-Arts. His assessment of these styles was accordingly vitriolic. Decades later, however, as he was in the midst of working his way out of the dead end he felt the glass-box tower had eventually become, Johnson could re-evaluate his position and write: "Those former enemies now look more interesting, more rich in associations, in metaphor, in decorative abundance, than the style which we espoused."

It was for pragmatic reasons as much as anything that Johnson/Burgee turned to art moderne sources at Post Oak. Unlike Pennzoil which was granted a little leeway, here the architects tackled speculative development precisely on its own terms. Money was the critical issue. "We thought of the cheapest things you could do," says Burgee, "and they were ribbon windows, setbacks and curved corners." That led them to the <u>haute élégance</u> of art moderne, which distinguishes these towers not only in shape but in material and color. Outside, the svelte towers are ringed in charcoal and silver, arranged in an intricately interlocking pattern of ribbons, dressed with the metallic sea-green reflections of the Texas sky. Surrounding the base is a single thickness of textured gray slate as plinth. Gray slate also paves the approaches, and the sumptuous materials and restrained palette continue on the inside. The lobby is also floored in slate, lined in light-gray marble, and the ceiling is finished in tiny gray tiles.

Altogether there are to be three towers, a retail building and a garage on a 17-acre site near major highways. The developer is the same Gerald D. Hines who developed Pennzoil, and Post Oak was actually begun earlier. All but the third tower and some of the landscaping have been completed in 1979. The arrangement of the complex is geared to automobile-dominated Houston. Post Oak I holds down one front corner, and Post Oak II the other. Between them is a triangle of lawn with a pool, and behind this open space will be Post Oak III. The three towers are of different shape, but of the same size and specifications.

The bits of baroque planning and sensual moderne elegance of Post Oak Central set it visually apart from the many clusters of office and mixed-use developments in the area. Refined taste and shrewd siting have been put into the skyline and the streetscape of Houston for the same bottom line as any other speculative building in town.

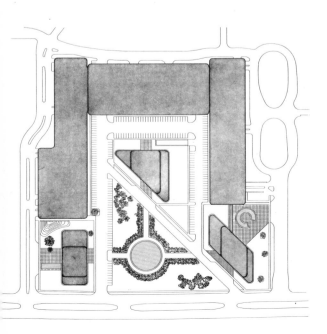

AVERY FISHER HALL INTERIOR

LINCOLN CENTER
NEW YORK, NEW YORK

Ever since Avery Fisher Hall opened in 1962 in Lincoln Center as the new home of the New York Philharmonic Orchestra, its acoustics were criticized. Musicians complained that they couldn't hear one another on stage, and audiences claimed that the sound was unevenly distributed throughout the hall. Three unsuccessful renovations led the owners to decide that they needed to gut the entire room and start over. For this they hired Johnson/Burgee (Johnson had designed the New York State Theater across the way) and acoustical consultant Cyril M. Harris.

Harris was dictator of all that affected sound, and he laid down a number of guidelines. The room was to be a conventional rectangular box (it had previously been shaped more like a juice bottle). It was to have three levels of balconies faced in convex curves to scatter sound. Wall and ceiling planes were to be broken, nonparallel and constructed to be as impervious to sound transmission as possible. Johnson/Burgee worked within these constraints. Visually the architects used them to realize two qualities: heightened intimacy, a serious need in a hall as large as 2,741 seats; and heightened ornament.

The color scheme is composed of variations on gold with gold plush chairs, warm ivory walls and ceiling, light-brown oak floors and gold-leaf balconies. The ceiling and walls are divided into a series of layers, marked by smooth bands that support can lights. Within each layer the ceiling breaks into strips of thin chevrons, and the walls fracture into equivalent striations breaking forward and back. Along the sides are three balconies with sections that step up slightly one behind another, like a series of private boxes. These are faced with rounded low walls, almost like moldings, covered with gold leaf and trimmed along the bottom with flickering filament lamps.

Not only do the multifaceted patterns scatter sound, they give a more responsive rhythm and scale to the otherwise vast room. The detailed fit between ceiling and walls binds them together in such a way that they seem to encase the seats. In front, the stage is wrapped in a diminishing series of gold and wood proscenium arches. The resulting foreshortened perspective rivets the audience's attention to the stage and brings it visually closer to the performers as well.

While more frenetic, the room is sumptuous and gracious in the manner of its eighteenth- and nineteenth-century predecessors, and is as contained as such a considerable hall can manage to be. The more critical issue, the acoustics, was received well by New York's music critics, and Avery Fisher Hall is finally acknowledged to be finished.

CENTURY CENTER

SOUTH BEND, INDIANA

Century Center and the simultaneous Fine Arts Center at Muhlenberg College are culminations of an idea that Johnson/Burgee has been developing through the years. The architects took the plan of a medieval European town with its central plaza and narrow little streets running off in various directions and use it as a model for a building. Sometimes they utilized only pieces of the model—just a court or a street. Sometimes, as at Pennzoil, they created mutations. At South Bend, the model was used directly, and in full, and unlike the earlier Corpus Christi museum, the plan is no longer subsumed within an overall building shape. It is truly a village, with buildings and streets and a plaza, only compact and roofed.

Originally the city had wanted to build separate buildings for a variety of cultural and convention facilities and to arrange them casually along the river. The architects suggested that the buildings be combined in a tight group, sharing not only walls but a common lobby or plaza. The group includes an industrial museum that displays such home-manufactured products as old Studebakers; a 25,000-square-foot convention center with private meeting rooms and banquet facilities; an art building with workshop, studio and gallery; and a 600-seat theater. The network of streets is clearly marked by its covering skylights. One street goes out to the parking lot, one to the bus stop, and the main entrance with its butterfly silhouette crosses the road to make a porte-cochere. Having picked up their passengers, the streets run through the center, passing all the specific buildings, and emptying into the plaza. Two of the streets actually continue beyond the other side, becoming bridges that span a little part of the river to an old artificial island.

The plaza, or common lobby, is the pivot of the design. Given Indiana's climate, it is roofed; given the building's configuration, it is triangular. It is the reception area for all the buildings. It can be used to mingle people from all the separate rooms or to serve each one in turn. One day it is set up for lunch for a convention group; later it might be used for cocktails for an art opening; and at night it is a theater lobby. Because it is a special place, it is distinguished architecturally from the other buildings and it has a different scale. While the other buildings are constructed in solid brick, the triangle is sheathed in metal and glass, and this court has a colossal order of white columns. The effect is that of an open square covered lightly by a tent. This village square, although sheltered from the elements, has a full glass wall that looks directly onto the river, where an old floodgate, stirring up the water, and a waterfall add visual drama.

Century Center organizes a variety of cultural and convention facilities as if they were separate buildings around a village square. Hallways are paved in brick and roofed in gabled skylights as interior streets. The triangular double-height court (above) is a common lobby.

The exterior expression of Century Center is one of highly articulated streets and receding brick boxes. The streets connect to the transportation systems outside. One leads in to the bus stop, one to the parking lot, and one forms an elaborate butterfly gable porte-cochere for the main entrance.

e pivot of the design is the central plaza,
pproached (at left) through the interior streets
 the grand staircase, which connects the
eet level with the river level (below).

FINE ARTS CENTER

MUHLENBERG COLLEGE
ALLENTOWN, PENNSYLVANIA

What was useful as an organizational device at Century Center has become the nucleus of the Muhlenberg College Fine Arts Center. A complex that contains theater, recital hall, art studios, gallery, English classrooms and faculty offices, it is arranged as a series of spaces and byways plugged into both sides of a wide, 200-foot-long skylit promenade. In 1955 Johnson wrote in a lament over the automobile: "It is time to re-create the street as a centering device, instead of the splitting device it has become ... Someday, people are again going to want to dance in village squares and when they want them, they will get them, and like Easter on Fifth Avenue, let the automobile take care of itself." Twenty years later, perhaps hedging their bets, the architects have put the street and village square inside, where the cars can't get at them.

Muhlenberg College, an old Lutheran-sponsored coeducational school with a history of excellence in math and science, had a college president who wished equal consideration for the humanities. He wanted not only to house the arts and letters but to make them integral to campus life. The architects made a building with a special kind of magnetism, beginning with an entrance that scoops visitors up from all directions and ushers them in. It is just the sort of arrangement at which Johnson/Burgee excels. The façade angles toward incoming cars as if it were their final destination. With proper regard for students on foot, the approach path is an open invitation to those leaving the student union across the street. The tall gabled entry presides over the area like the meeting house over a New England village. Although the upper section is glazed all the way to the top, a thick black grid of mullions and muntins marks it as wall.

Inside is a cultural market street. The brick paving continues underneath, daylight filters in through the skylight, and along both sides are white-painted brick buildings. Within these buildings are the theater, gallery, recital hall, corridors of classrooms and offices. But the street is essentially a street—with one major and important exception. All along it, on either side, are irregularly sized triangular plazas—some only large enough to hold a few wicker chairs, one big enough to double as theater lobby. The nooks and crannies, formed by slicing the galleria through the building at a 45-degree angle, are edged in carpeted benches and were left unprogramed in the hope that students would study and chat and hang out along the street, accidentally seeing the art shows and hearing the concert rehearsals.

As the street slopes gently down the incline, it grows into a triangular village square, suddenly three stories high and enclosed urbanistically with a bridge over one side, a stair to another and a café across. On the other side of the bridge, which separates it nicely from the square, is a small foyer, and beyond is the back door, a calmer version of the front entrance.

What began as a humanities center became a real street and town square with the simplest of elements: sunlight, niches and a parade. Students with or without scheduled classes gather there, and the openness of the galleria makes it a convenient location for receptions, formal dinners and community events. The president's ambition has been realized, and architectural institutional clichés refuted.

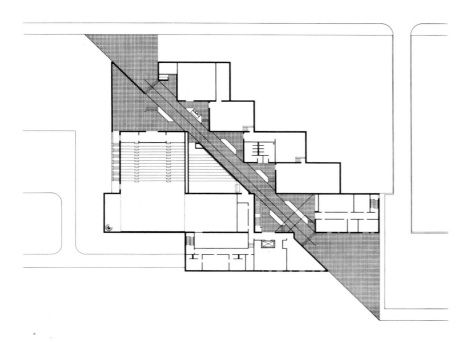

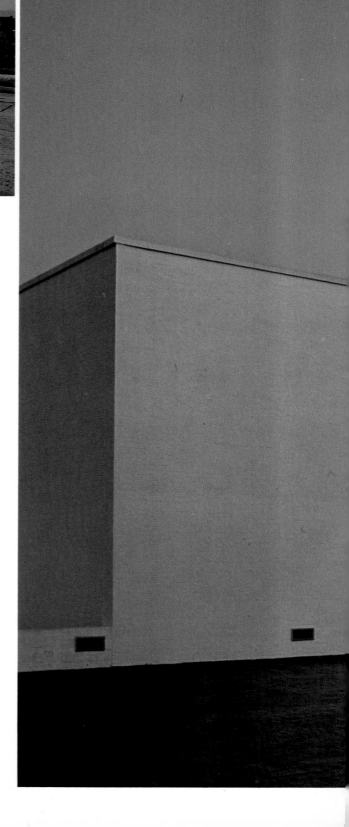

The Fine Arts Center places its greatest emphasis on entry. The gesture is intentionally symbolic, for the center was meant to introduce arts and letters as an area of serious concern to a college that had long specialized in the sciences.

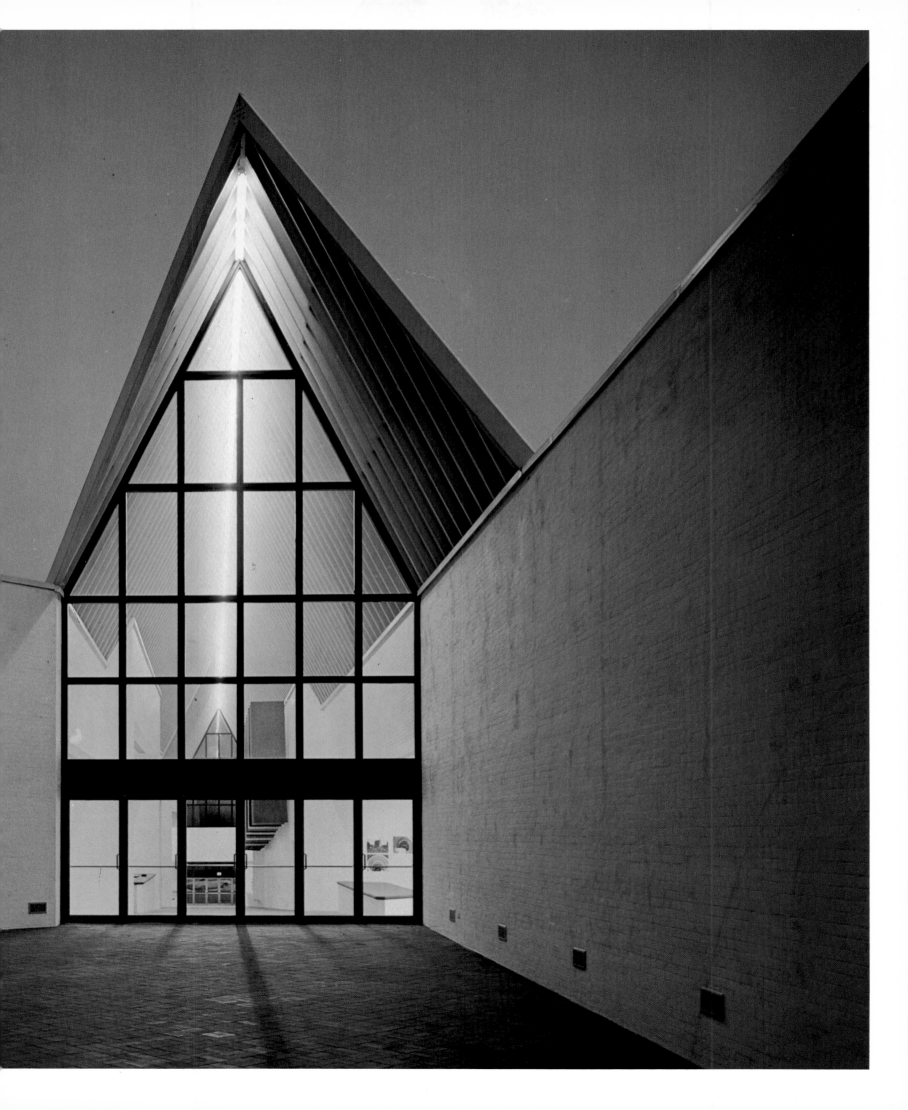

The activities of the Fine Arts Center open off a wide internal skylight street. Along the street are triangular niches of various sizes to encourage students to spend time in the building, and at the end, a town square. The view from the bridge (right) back toward the front door.

GENERAL AMERICAN LIFE INSURANCE COMPANY

ST. LOUIS, MISSOURI

Having gained a reputation in corporate building, Johnson/Burgee was offered more commissions, this one for a small headquarters building in downtown St. Louis. The site was prominent: near the famous Saarinen arch and across a proposed mall from Sullivan's landmark Wainwright Building. Though the company employs only four hundred people and did not want to build rental space, it was concerned with establishing a distinct presence in a highly visible area.

Johnson/Burgee gave impact to a building that did not need to be more than three stories high, much as it had at Pennzoil, by creating a series of clear architectural pieces in locked combat with one another and also a clearly suggested whole. A square building, it is chopped in two, along the diagonal, with one half left on the ground and the other lifted up three stories in the air. Inserted between is a narrow slab of brick (containing fire stairs) holding the straining halves apart. Ever urbanistic, the architects let the low half face toward a sports stadium, the higher toward office buildings.

Cut out of the center of this block is a huge cylinder. Both square and cylinder are sheathed in glass—in this case a proto-plaid challenge to standard curtain wall. While the large grey metal columns of the square continue through the rotunda (of which it is a part), slender white columns punctuate the glass edges of the cylinder, both down on the ground in front of the plaza on one side and up in the air in front of the terrace on the other. The approach is diagonal, lined in columns, and thrown in shadow by the half building above.

Inside the huge cylinder, the ceiling rises to 107 feet, sunlight streaming in from across the way. There are two elaborate sculptural staircases that whip back and forth. The grey columns continue to the center and to the elevators. Johnson is fond of saying that in modern buildings it is at the elevator where the procession ends. But here, borrowing a trick from John Portman, Johnson/Burgee keeps it going. Each of the elevators has a side that has been bent out and sheathed in glass, for a dramatic ride up the center of the galleria. From the elevator lobbies, bridges cross over to the office spaces.

The tensions of the exterior geometry—parts against whole, cube against cylinder, glass against masonry—are continued inside. The rotunda is lined in brick, the offices in glass. Some elements are rounded; the rest are decidedly angular. The elevator lobbies are octagonal, but the shafts themselves push forward, breaking the lines and complicating the pattern. The balconies are circular but cut forward where the bridges connect. There are more intricacies. The solid-brick staircases are startlingly white underneath. Each wall of brick is lined at top and bottom in bricks set on edge to distinguish these from the running bond of the mass. The elevator shafts are even interrupted by such a layer to demark each floor. Much of the procession is rendered in details that have become identified with Johnson/Burgee: rows of recessed lights, corduroy-like metal columns, fat cylindrical bridge railings, and light-colored sash wherever the effect desired is invisibility.

The import is not only that there has been a consistently developing Johnson/Burgee vocabulary in office design but that the St. Louis commission was an opportunity the firm had not had before. It is not just skin and lobby. It is an interior. And that extends to the furnishings as well. The typical office space is open landscaping—a sophisticated basic white with accents of bright green, orange, yellow, red, blue, like a Calder print; and special places show Johnson/Burgee's taste for rich materials: brown ultrasuede walls, brass and granite furniture, and specially commissioned artwork.

The cylindrical galleria is a monumental lobby, open to the full six stories of the building and flooded with daylight. The circulation elements within, such as the stairs and elevators, are given sculptural form. A duality is suggested between the heavy red brick of the drum and the lightweight structure of the bridges.

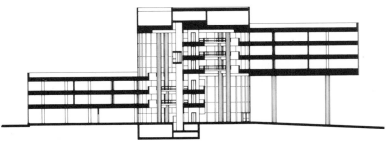

In an effort to give a small building a large visual impact, the architects sliced it in two, raised one half off the ground and carved a huge cylinder out of the middle. Along the center of the building there is a narrow slice of brick wall separating the halves. The curtain wall is a proto-plaid, one of the many experiments Johnson/Burgee has undertaken with the standard glass curtain-wall formula.

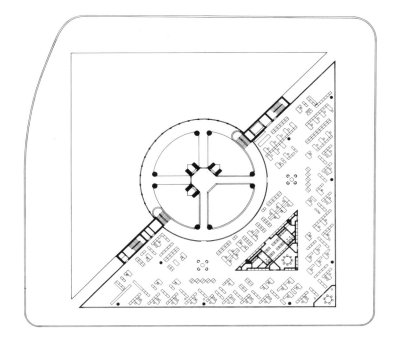

One of the sources for General American Life's galleria was the atrium hotels of John Portman. From them Johnson/Burgee adapted the notion of open vertical space, glass-sided elevators and suspended stacked elevator lobbies in the center connected by bridges to the offices on the outer ring.

THANKS-GIVING SQUARE

DALLAS, TEXAS

At Thanks-Giving Square, Johnson/Burgee had nothing like the area they worked with in Fort Worth. Instead, there was a tiny triangle, approximately one acre, in the middle of Dallas' banking and commercial center. A charitable religious foundation had purchased the site for a chapel and a chapel garden to commemorate world thanksgiving. The architects took this small area, which was surrounded by skyscrapers, sunk it appreciably, ringed it with a low wall and drew on their by now extensive vocabulary to give it place.

The main approach begins at the narrowest corner, with the needle point filled with planting. Visitors are funneled in from the edges and through the carillon—three bronze bells hung high on simple scaffolding—which forms the first gateway. Rippled concrete walls washed with water form the second gateway. The garden itself is an agitated geometry with angular wedges fitted tight against one another. There are only four materials: trapezoids of soft green grass; white concrete; thoroughfares and plazas of a coarse aggregate of tan cement and red stone; and water. Down the center a path descends, paralleled by a foaming river. To each side are miniature events: a viewing terrace, a street leading out of town, a sacred grove framed against a waterfall. At the bottom is the center of activity, a town square with trails splintering off back to the street and with a panoply of water effects. The huge white-water slide is the main attraction, cascading from a smooth lake down a stone baffle that breaks up the water into little rivulets and rapids, worked into a froth at its narrow bottom.

The focus of the square is the spiral chapel. High and white, it is the one element that is visible from outside the walls. Inside, it is a simple room with a few folding chairs and an altar of two shapes, a white Carrara-marble cube on a circle of red granite. The drama is created by the roof, which, spiraling into the air above worshipers, is webbed in stained glass. The exterior of this spiral cannot be ascended, but the ninth-century minaret near Samara that served as a model could be climbed, and from its pinnacle the faithful were called to prayer. Here that aural device is translated into a 92-foot-high visual one.

The chapel garden is connected to Dallas' underground street of shops through an entrance off the little town square. Farther down, although there is no opening, the architects inserted a skylight (sunken in the planting bed at the corner), which throws daylight onto the underground passage. Through the glass can be seen the bell tower, a reminder not only of where one is but of where one might be. It is all part of the procession: the hints from a distance that this might really be something not to miss, the paths that gradually reveal one part of the story after another, and the center itself, a core of activity that denies its size to provide respite, physical and spiritual, from downtown Dallas.

Thanks-Giving Square is a chapel and a chapel garden dedicated to world thanksgiving. The carillon tower rises at one end (opposite page, top left), and the white chapel at the other (opposite page, top right; interior, left). The garden is a series of water effects in a park setting highlighted by a huge white-water slide.

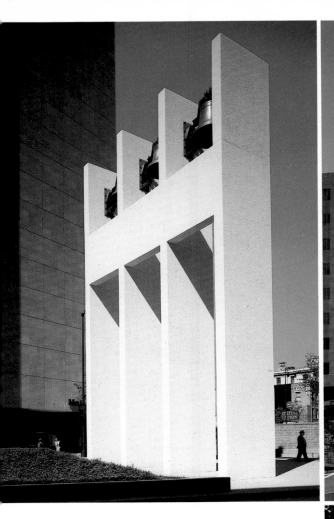

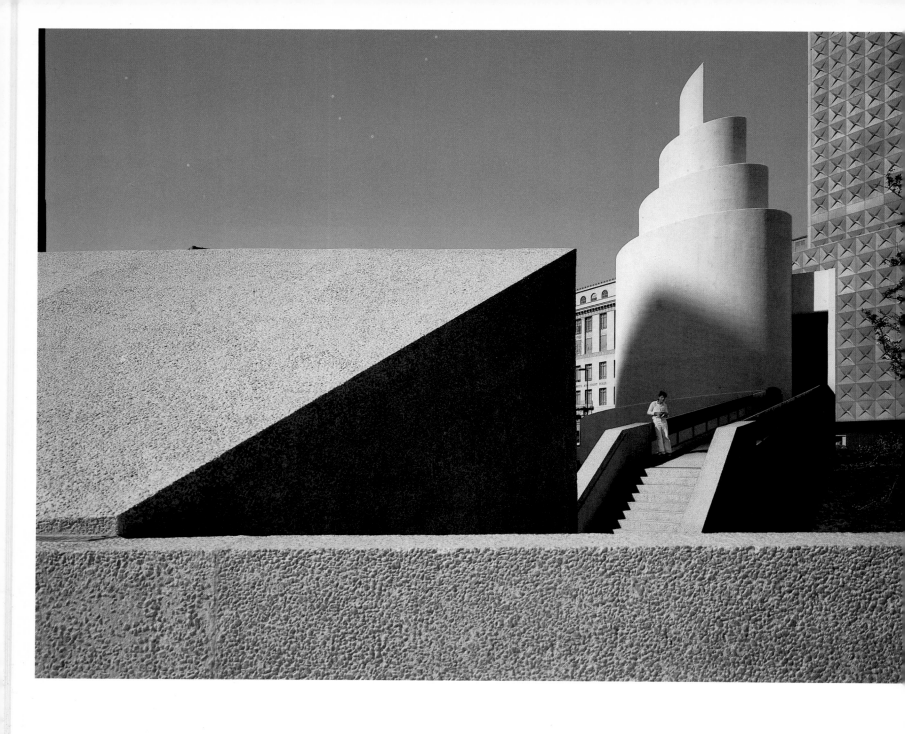

The form of the chapel was suggested by a ninth-century minaret near Samara. The spiral of the chapel roof is inlaid with stained glass made by artisans in Chartres.

80 FIELD POINT ROAD

GREENWICH, CONNECTICUT

Although a small, speculative office in suburban Greenwich, 80 Field Point Road is not unrelated to the firm's larger efforts. It is a forceful affront to the ubiquitous box, and it also incorporates a number of the more spectacular natural-light effects Johnson/Burgee developed in previous projects, albeit here in miniature. The building sits on a tree-lined street dotted with low square brick office buildings and an occasional large old house. It conforms in scale and color to its commercial neighbors while making a few self-conscious improvements. Its solid surfaces are of stately red granite; its cars are parked discreetly; and its driveway and sidewalk are finished in red concrete aggregate, forming a total site composition.

In plan, it is a rectangular box with a curved section gashed out of it. The side with the gouge faces the street. The granite around the cut continues just far enough forward to prevent its retreating into the niceties of a mere arc. Despite the aggressiveness of the geometry, the curve faces to the street, sheathed in white-gridded glass. The box has been scuttled, front and back defined, and distinctness from neighbors assured. The client for the building, a newsprint concern which occupies the top floor, expressed interest in having its own private elevator. This the architects provided, using the free-standing pier to re-establish the building edge which is missing, and which serves as a sign in Venturi-like highway vernacular.

The gabled skylit thoroughfare at Muhlenberg or South Bend shows up as a tiny bridge from private elevator to top-floor offices. As at Morningside House, the horizontality of the low, rather squat building is the design cue for the exterior.

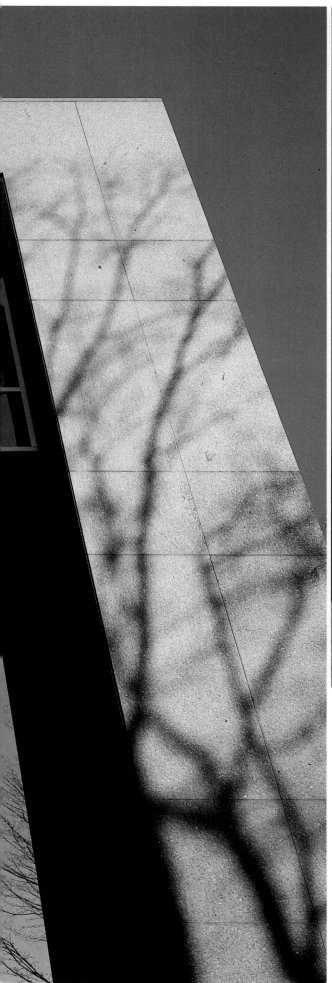

The breaking of the box is particularly aggressive at 80 Field Point Road, where the architects have gashed a large curve out of it. On the third floor, for the offices of the building's owner, they have introduced smaller versions of Pennzoil's canted roof and Muhlenberg's gabled skylit street for natural lighting.

1001
FIFTH AVENUE
FAÇADE

NEW YORK, NEW YORK

At 1001 Fifth Avenue, as at the Boston Public Library addition, Johnson/Burgee entered the realm of literal historical allusion in the interests of architectural neighborliness. This time it was the neighbors who brought it up. The site had been a touchy local issue for some time, ever since a developer assembled it, tore down a couple of town houses over protest, and then declared bankruptcy. When H. J. Kalikow Company bought the property, hired architect Philip Birnbaum to design an apartment tower and filed for building permits, it ran into organized community opposition and an injunction. In complicated negotiations among local groups, developer, judge, lawyers, civic landmark authorities and an architecture professor, a compromise was reached. Johnson/Burgee was hired to give Birnbaum's design a different face, a façade that would be more in keeping with the landmark 1911 McKim, Mead & White Italian palazzo to one side, the 1903 French town house to the other, and New York's Metropolitan Museum of Art across the street.

It was not possible to redesign the apartment units, redefine the project or prevent its towering over its neighbors. What the architects did was sift through a historical kit of parts and adapt some to a kind and size of commission that could only be modern—as Louis Sullivan, John Russell Pope, Raymond Hood and countless others had done before them. But since it was some decades since the 1920s revivalists—the last guiltless fanciers of applied ornament—and since it was a highly restricted endeavor, they did so a little differently.

At the base, where the concerned neighbors and out-of-town visitors walk by, the design is seriously neoclassical. Rusticated limestone in the same fashion as its McKim, Mead & White neighbor, glass entrance outlined in semicircular stone molding, and doorway flanked by antique lanterns, it blends well with much of stately New York. Yet homogenation is not the point and is carefully avoided, most insistently by moldings which stop short of the building's edges. From there, the building becomes less and less serious. As if to declare itself as a last-minute touch-up, it defers to anything and everything. The string courses continue to stop short of the corners. The vertical strips of spec bay windows tear right through the stone façade without even an attempt at resolution. The roof of the adjacent landmark pokes into the living room of the apartment next door.

The top is outright mimicry. Its sides bend in, but its front doesn't bend back, so at the least it is a chamfered false front held up by struts impersonating a mansard. But it doesn't stop there. At the base of the cant is a triple string course standing in for an absent cornice, a symbolic gesture one might let pass if the windows didn't shove on through, insolently outlined in limestone molding.

The McKim, Mead & White palazzo being the declared prototype for the design, the architects borrowed that building's horizontal banding, along with its rustication. But it is the little town house on the other side that the final building most resembles, with its vertical proportions, its low base, tall bay-windowed shaft and quasi-mansard roof.

But 1001 Fifth is a special brand of borrowing. It was built in 1979, as a last-ditch effort at sensitivity to its context for a developer whose profits depended on a completely different kind of building than its neighbors; for a city that allowed it to tower over those neighbors; and for neighbors that hadn't been bothered by any such delicate considerations when it was their turn to be new. Johnson/Burgee's 1001 Fifth Avenue is reasonably neighborly, but it is not innocent.

STUDIO THEATER

KENNEDY CENTER
WASHINGTON, D.C.

As at Avery Fisher Hall, the firm was commissioned to insert an auditorium into an already existing building. At the Kennedy Center, however, it was not a malfunctioning concert hall that was to be replaced, but a theater that had never been completed. Money ran out during the construction of Edward Durell Stone's Kennedy Center for the Performing Arts. All that was built of this studio theater was its shell. By the time, eight years later, that the Japanese government donated $3 million to finish the room, the original architect had died and Johnson/Burgee was hired. Cyril M. Harris was again the acoustical consultant, and his insistence on broken planes, absorptive and reflective materials and such were the departure points for the design.

What did not concern Harris and what seems most startlingly different from Avery Fisher Hall is the thirties night-club quality of color. This intimate little auditorium is a moderne mood piece in pink, purple and shimmering silver. The foyer is a jarring, excited mélange of purplish-blue walls, red-violet carpet and dusty-pink modular seating. Its darkish indigo gives way to the sparkling slinkiness of the theater itself, with the dusty pink enveloping the whole room. Within are set rows of plush plum-color seating.

The ivory and gold hues of Avery Fisher Hall have been replaced with the sultry luminosity of purples, pinks and silver in this more casual room of 500 seats for drama and chamber music. Johnson/Burgee came to color rather late in its career and turns to it to replace the sensuality found, when it is financially feasible, with expensive materials.

The dusty-pink planes of ceiling and walls are bent in a sawtooth pattern that progresses from lumbering to staccato as it moves forward. Within the notches formed on the side walls are placed silver columns, short and fat at the top of the steeply raked auditorium, gradually taller and more slender toward the front. From their bases, hidden sources throw light upward.

The columns people the walls as do the tiers of boxes at Avery Fisher Hall, providing a rhythm that does not stop where the stage begins but continues through the series of proscenium arches, each one progressively smaller.

The result is a foreshortened perspective as at Avery Fisher Hall, beginning at the very back with the wide chevrons of ceiling and walls, continuing through the ever narrowing bends and ever slimming, more closely set columns, along the ever diminishing prosceniums onto the stage. It is a perspective effect that encompasses the entire theater.

This effect is amplified by holding the columns just short of the ceiling—a kind of Miesian truth-in-structure. The ceiling and walls become a one-piece cover in which the columns, along with stage and seating, merely stand in place. The enclosure holds the room intact, the perspective brings audience and performers closer together, and it is all done with a taut economy of means. A few elements—barely distinguishable colors accented with silver, hidden light and jagged edges—are manipulated, appropriately theatrically, to create a room of intimacy and sophisticated elegance.

While a number of Johnson/Burgee projects have been considered major buildings, it is the architects' latest series of designs that have catapulted them into the center of public attention and into the center of heated debates over architectural values. The new work is called alternately a breakthrough, an aberration or an outrage. What is as interesting as the partisan arguments is the sense in which these projects can be seen not as brilliant or perverse deflections but as integral developments. (The three projects illustrated here are either under construction or about to be.)

Most unusual as a building type is the Crystal Cathedral for the Reverend Dr. Robert H. Schuller, a drive-in evangelist whose singular career has taken him from atop a refreshment stand at an outdoor movie theater to minister of television's internationally syndicated <u>Hour of Power</u> and what he calls his "22-acre shopping center for Jesus Christ" in Garden Grove, California. When the persuasiveness of his "possibility thinking" outgrew the Richard Neutra-designed ecclesiastical complex, he went to Johnson/Burgee for a bigger church: big enough for 4,000 people. Further, Schuller insisted on glass. "If a two-by-four comes between your eyeball and the changing edge of a cloud," he said, "something is lost. I want to tie the religious experience to nature, and if people see the sky, and the traffic on the freeway too, that's good—it means that religion is not divorced from reality."

The architects drew on their considerable experience with crystalline shapes and glass-covered galleries, as well as with auditoriums. The idea is to get people as close to the performance as possible, so, as John Burgee puts it, "we squished the nave and pulled out the trancept." Translated into primary geometries, it became a four-pointed star, with free-standing balconies in three points and the chancel in the fourth. The connection with reality is maintained through ten thousand panes of glass hung on a space-frame scaffolding like a gigantic transparent tent. From the outside its quartz-like facets shimmer in one another's mirrored surfaces and reflective pond below. Inside, the mood is hushed, the filtered light lending a cool expectant atmosphere.

The congregation enters from the points of the star, under the low balconies and into the explosion of the center space—higher, wider and longer than Paris' Notre Dame. Down the central aisle is a procession of fountains that gush as people enter, but come to a sudden lull just before the Reverend speaks. All eyes are focused front, not only to the highest point, but to the marble the color of fire, to the oak choir screening and to the organ pipes splintered and hung in cubist abstraction. Those worshipers still in their cars listen to Schuller on the radio, watch him through the glass and wait for the moments when he walks out the Cape Canaveral doors on the side of the stage to address himself to them.

The architects' new skyscrapers have been greeted with the greatest shock. "It's not only that we're breaking the rules," says Burgee, "we're breaking the rules for the same kind of building that they were written for." While many critics were prepared to honor the designers for their earlier departures from the conventional glass box, they were prepared only to go so far as minimalist sculpture. The architects, however, have found themselves, as did American architects of the 1920s, "roaming history at will." Their consciously revivalist designs—a logical development from the Boston Public Library—are now presented without the armature of paying respect to a neighboring landmark. "We yearn for some richness," exclaims Johnson, in a justification of the new finials but relevant to other elements as well, "for something that marks out one building from another."

AT&T in midtown Manhattan is marked out by a neoclassical curtain wall, drawing on Sullivan's Guaranty Building, Brunelleschi's Pazzi Chapel, and McKim, Mead & White among others, but more abstract, disjointed and abrupt than any of its precedents. With them it shares the clarity of tripartite order and symmetry; the grandeur of stone (a rose-gray granite carved to heighten the play of light and shadow); and recognizable forms such as a coffered vault and broken pediment. But to these it adds a different sensibility, one of aloof annotation and satire, where a doorway ornament can become the roof of a 660-foot building or unrelated window patterns can coexist by mere juxtaposition.

It also adds a very non-1920s concept, in fact a concept which is by no means always associated with revivalism. This concept—a respect for the particular char-

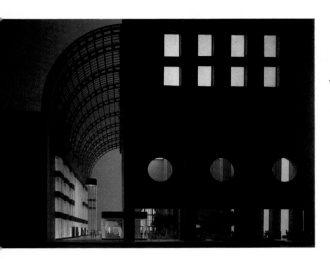

WORKS IN PROGRESS

AT&T
NEW YORK, NEW YORK

PPG
PITTSBURGH, PENNSYLVANIA

CRYSTAL CATHEDRAL
GARDEN GROVE, CALIFORNIA

acteristics of a place (genius loci) and belief in the value of regionalism—is very much in line with the reactions against the internationalism of orthodox modernism. What adds a wry twinge is that the contexts to which Johnson/Burgee finds itself responding are America's imitations of European architecture from a time when America lacked pride in either its own traditions or its potential to develop any. None of this, however, reduces the force of the argument that the context, once there, is worth maintaining. For New York skyscrapers, context can mean neoclassicism as much as modernism. In this case, context also means AT&T's former neoclassical headquarters.

The street floor of AT&T is a compromise between corporate identity and public domain. Madison Avenue, on which the building faces, is a shopping street, and the city planning office was anxious that it not be interrupted. But AT&T didn't want a front door sandwiched between a drug store and a lingerie shop. The architects lifted the whole building 60 feet in the air. Only the central bay at ground level is actual building, a minimal foyer with special elevators to the real lobby above. The remainder is a hypostyle hall, open-air but shielded from the elements, furnished with café tables and kiosks. Just behind is a shop-lined galleria, and above the shops, a science exhibit hall.

It is a simple space but not a still one. The floor is made of granite mosaic in a pattern derived from Lutyens. The curved beams of the galleria's skylight are a literal copy of those at Milan. Even the effect of the drawings has been startling; it has been called nostalgia, black humor and obscurantism. In a sense these are all true, but the real point is that it is also the architects' first real searching for a whole new level of richness—not just of material, not just of silhouette, not even just of street life, but the richness at fingertip scale that makes the architecture of the past so compelling.

Not long after AT&T came the design for a new headquarters for PPG in Pittsburgh. As PPG is a major manufacturer of architectural glass, it was clear that the building would not be faced in granite. What interested the architects was how mirrored glass resembled stone as an architectural material, since it appears solid and not transparent, as does clear glass. If AT&T's articulation is neoclassical, PPG's is neogothic, with that same time-machine range from Barry and Pugin's Houses of Parliament to Saarinen's CBS Building. Along the façades are close-set piers, alternating diamond and square sections. When the re-reflections turn one facet black, the next will be white and the whole row will flicker back and forth. The piers grow into a gothic forest of spikes and spires and crowns at the top. At the bottom they split and bundle into pointed archways. The architects make their genius loci argument, referring to the gothic-inspired University of Pittsburgh and Richardson's romanesque courthouse as examples of local character.

As the five-block site was urban-renewal property and an attempt to extend the resurgence of the famous Golden Triangle into an adjacent neighborhood, attention was devoted to encouraging pedestrian activity at street level. Behind the forty-four-story tower is a gabled skylit winter garden with café tables and small food kiosks scattered among the plants. Borrowing from Minneapolis, a glass bridge connects to Golden Triangle Park across the way. The formal entrance of the tower faces a square plaza, surrounded by five-story buildings in the same general style as the tower, and lined on the interior with a covered arcade and rows of shops inspired by Bologna.

To Johnson/Burgee, there are three things that can be done to rescue the high rise from banality: give it shape, give it texture and pack in activity at the bottom. It is what they have been doing for years. Where they find themselves now, and it is not unwitting, is in a kind of replay of the controversy of the Chicago Tribune Competition of 1921. In a period when the spoils of the modernists are being subjected to disappointed scrutiny, it is hardly surprising that architects should be tempted to relive the last great victory of the masters of architectural tradition. What makes Johnson/Burgee particularly important is that for them it was not a moral battle then and it is not one now. The question is not historical trappings versus bold new geometries, stone versus glass, symmetry versus asymmetry. They like it all. To them the issues are what they have always been: tactile, kinesthetic, visual, intellectual. "What keeps you going," says Johnson, "is the kick you get out of making a shape and a space."

CHRONOLOGY
(dates are those of completion)

1972

ART MUSEUM OF SOUTH TEXAS Corpus Christi, Texas
Associated architects: Barnstone & Aubry

BURDEN HALL

Harvard Graduate School of Business Administration, Boston, Massachusetts

NEUBERGER MUSEUM State University of New York, Purchase, New York

1973

I.D.S. CENTER Minneapolis, Minnesota
Joint venture architects: Edward F. Baker Associates, Inc.

ADDITION, BOSTON PUBLIC LIBRARY Boston, Massachusetts
Joint venture architects: Architects Design Group, Inc.

1974

NIAGARA FALLS CONVENTION CENTER Niagara Falls, New York

1975

FORT WORTH WATER GARDEN Fort Worth, Texas

MORNINGSIDE HOUSE New York, New York

1976

PENNZOIL PLACE Houston, Texas
Associated architects: Wilson, Morris, Crain & Anderson

POST OAK CENTRAL I Houston, Texas
Associated architects: Fitzgerald Associates

INTERIOR, AVERY FISHER HALL Lincoln Center, New York, New York

1977

CENTURY CENTER South Bend, Indiana

FINE ARTS CENTER Muhlenberg College, Allentown, Pennsylvania
Associated architects: Coston, Wallace & Watson

GENERAL AMERICAN LIFE INSURANCE COMPANY St. Louis, Missouri

THANKS-GIVING SQUARE Dallas, Texas

1978

80 FIELD POINT ROAD Greenwich, Connecticut

FAÇADE, 1001 FIFTH AVENUE New York, New York

POST OAK CENTRAL II Houston, Texas
Associated architects: Fitzgerald Associates

STUDIO THEATER, KENNEDY CENTER Washington, D.C.

1979
UNDER CONSTRUCTION

APARTMENT GROUP Isfahan, Iran

NATIONAL CENTER FOR THE PERFORMING ARTS Bombay, India

A.T.&T. HEADQUARTERS New York, New York

CIVIC CENTER Peoria, Illinois

CRYSTAL CATHEDRAL
Garden Grove Community Church, Garden Grove, California

GRAPHIC CREDITS
ART DIRECTOR: ROBERT SCUDELLARI
PROJECT DIRECTOR: PETER MOLLMAN
PRODUCED BY CHANTICLEER PRESS, INC.
PRINTED AND BOUND BY AMILCARE PIZZI, S.P.A., MILAN, ITALY